Mosquito Nirva

811.
54
Pla   Plantos, Ted
           Mosquito Nirvana

Y

LENNOX & ADDINGTON
COUNTY PUBLIC
LIBRARY

Mosquito Nirvana

Ted Plantos

Wolsak and Wynn . Toronto

Copyright © Ted Plantos, 1993

All rights reserved.
No part of this book may be reproduced, stored in a retrieval system, or transmitted, in any form, by any means, electronic or mechanical, without permission in writing from the publisher, except by a reviewer who may quote brief passages in a review. In case of photocopying or other reprographic copying, a licence from Canadian Reprography Collective (CANCOPY), 214 King Street West, Suite 312, Toronto, ON M5H 3S6 is required. US requests should be sent to Copyright Clearance Center, Inc., 27 Congress Street, Salem, MA 01970.

Some of these poems have appeared in: Arc, Greenfield Review, Canadian Author & Bookman, Waves, Pittsburgh Quarterly, Canadian Forum, Anthos, Dandelion and Poetry Canada Review.

Cover design by Rob Malyon
Author's photograph by Edward Plantos
Typeset in Palatino, printed in Canada by
The Coach House Printing Co., Toronto.

The author acknowledges with gratitude the assistance of the Ontario Arts Council during the writing of several poems in this collection.

Special thanks to Carol Malyon, John B. Lee and Ed Plantos for their editorial comments.

The publishers gratefully acknowledge support by The Canada Council and The Ontario Arts Council.

Wolsak and Wynn Publishers Ltd.
Don Mills Post Office Box 316
Don Mills, Ontario, Canada, M3C 2S7

Canadian Cataloguing in Publication Data
Plantos, Ted, 1943-
  Mosquito Nirvana
Poems.
ISBN 0-919897-36-3
I. Title.

PS8591.L36M68 1993   C811'.54   C93-093913-1
PR9199.3.P53M68 1993

for Marty Gervais

LENNOX & ADDINGTON
COUNTY PUBLIC
LIBRARY

CONTENTS

THE FLIP SIDE OF NIRVANA

MOSQUITO PICKLES

MOSQUITO PICKLES

Dusty bottles
on the store shelves
He dreams of ice
or cold orange soda
in his throat, uncapped
among molasses, flour sacks
and milk foamed to a head of cream

Humid flowers waver
Bees circle themselves
in constant humming

There are rivers eddying everywhere
He finds one in his pocket
with a treasure chest of five nickels,
two green and orange marbles
and a pearl-handled pocket knife
buried in sand

He sees another river overhead,
bass bathing in blue current
Casting out to the sky, he hauls in
his day's dinner of dream

And another river underfoot,
back road down
to the shore of highway

Belly flat
on the flattened grass,
his face swims in the trout stream
He sees himself pebbled, floating there
and reaches in for a handful of eyes
to drink chilled, their blue grape taste

Sun on the dump,
the smell of tins
yesterday emptied to plates:

rusted metal, sodden newspapers,
jagged misted glass,
and today's rats
in their garbage euphoria

A half-ton truck pulls off
the gravel rock-smacking road
A boy in the back,
highway wind in his hair,
crunches a melting chocolate bar,
lets the wrapper fly into a cornfield

Whatever happened to green
among the sun's paled trees,
off where afternoon settles
in the sweat-heaped fields

Mosquitoes get into his sandwich
on the porch on the table on the plate:

mosquito and cheese,
mosquito pickles,
homemade mosquito lemonade,
mosquito ice cubes,
mosquito-stung mouth,
mosquitoes for lunch
and flies in his cake at dinner
circle pink icing, circle the spoon

— angel pink-iced fly cake,
and now the hind-leg hopping crickets
rub their wings in moon grass
while the dogs yelp at passing stars

That night, a river takes him away,
row-boating past lily pads,
white lilies on the satin swift water

THE GIANT'S TREASURE

In the back seat, he bites into a tomato

Mom's up front and John's driving

He can still smell gasoline
from when John filled up
He likes to smell gasoline

On sundays at picnics
his favourite smells
are gasoline hard boiled eggs
and the air off lakes

The tomato is bigger than his hand
He holds it in both and eats
Juices sweet, warming his throat

John is a nice man
He owns a store and lets him help out
It's not a candy store,
but John *has* candies
Boxes of all kinds and colours
Red licorice is best
Next is Wildfire chocolate bars

People come from work to John's store
Some ask for credit, but most pay

He stares at the half-eaten tomato
and thinks, next to apples tomatoes are best

John likes salt on his tomatoes, and also pepper
Mom likes tomato sandwiches with hot tea

Tomatoes are best warm,
he remembers John telling Mom
— and he's sure Mom said
>   *No, tomatoes are better cold*

His tomato is warm from being
in a bag on the back seat
with the sun coasting by

He opens the cooler, flattens his palms
on a block of ice, and shivers

The sky is gold like a giant's treasure
when they stop by a lake
Gold with lots of blue, and birds flying in it
Gulls, John calls them

John shows him how to skip stones on the water,
and he skips some more than five times

He'll never forget John telling him
flat stones skip best, tossed sidearm
flat along the line of water,
jumping waves and skimming the sun

Still gold, the giant's treasure at the end of day
Gold with some pink in it lighting up the trees
like sparkles from a magic wand

He thinks he saw this place in a fairytale once
Or maybe it was make-believe

Mom and John weren't in that story
That's why this place is best

THE OLD WOMEN OF GERRARD STREET

Two old women lead the dirt-faced child into their dining room
He is happy that neither attempt to remove
his hard-earned dirt with a scratchy face cloth,
or moralize on the virtues of soap
They take him as is:

spotted face, lips red from a cherry popsicle,
one bruised knee out of jeans
torn from climbing a wire fence,
and running shoes unlaced
to make neat flapping sounds when he ran
He takes the women as they are:

trusts those laced eyes and powdered smiles
Their grey calms him, accepts him, wants his company

One woman plays piano while the other
tends to the kettle hissing steam
in a kitchen that smells like tangerines
He remembers that smell from Christmas:

tangerines walnuts oranges in bowls on the table,
ripe for grabbing on the way out his snowbound door

Standing next to the pianist,
he squints through the stained glass window
and wonders why the world
doesn't change colours more often
A world of blue would be fun:

blue cars blue wagons blue cookies blue bicycles
blueberry jello blue horses blue people blue everything
And the next day could be yellow All yellow:

not just lemons and grapefruits,
but cakes and cowboy hats as well

She carries the teapot to the stove,
pours fog from varnished hands,
and speaks to him as if he were a person:
    We'll have cake with our tea

He doesn't ask what kind of cake, but wants to know

    Surprise cake Close your eyes and don't look, she tells him

He closes his eyes around imagined
mounds of cherry-splattered vanilla icing

    You can open them now, she says

Icing melts from his eyes
like peaks of rooftop snow on a sunny day
But the cherries stay:

green and red ones embedded with citrus in dark fruit cake
His eyes narrow on the pink-flowered plate she hands him

    Christmas cake, he says, and plucks
a chopped walnut from the brandy-moistened pastry,
crunching it like nothing-at-all for teeth
that can take on peanut brittle, toffee
and that rope someone tied to his dog's hind leg
Nothing-at-all for teeth that can double up
on double bubble gum and chewy wax lips

He plucks fruit from the cake
a piece at a time, leaving little craters
like the women's eyes that recede
into mahogany, and candles taller
than the ones he saw at mass on Sunday
when he sneaked with Gordon
out the back door after Father McKillop
had blessed their presence in heaven's head count

He hates church incense,
but the old women smell of lilacs:

lilacs and lemon oil and wrinkled sunlight
And that's all right

He watches the two together tipping their cups
into saucers they sip from
When he tells them his cup is empty,
both speak as one with two sets of ruby lips:
>*Oh no, dear, your cup is quite full*

He tips it to show them,
and the pianist snatches the cup from his hand,
holds it to her face and squints
A long finger traces the gold rim
Eyes on the tea leaves inside, and voice saying:
>*See Do you see the horse running in your cup?*

He leans across the table and looks
>*Yes, I see his ears too ... and I see a hand*

The pianist pats his wrist
>*That's my hand, dear Now let me read your fortune*

He wants to know what his fortune has to do with a horse

>*It means you have a strong future*

Future? His mother will be calling him for dinner soon
Does the pianist see tomato soup in his future?

>*No, I see lamb chops Lamb chops with mint,*
>*the way you like them ... and mashed potatoes*
>*You better hurry home They're heating on the stove*

His laces flap down the stairs

He stops, looking back
at the landing where they stand
His eyes thank them
for the fruitcake, tea and his future

You're quite welcome, dear, they say

THE LONE RANGER SOCIAL CLUB

Under the railroad bridge, under
our feet bared to cautious stepping,
we looked down between battered crossbeam ties
at the Don — that tramping river
going nowhere under our balancing act, under
the sun making rivers down backs
that knew only the burden of carrying
schoolbooks home from the pool hall

We were the great adventure,
heroes of a kind that stick together
like bubblegum and wax lips
when we burst onto the scene, any scene,
with our heads in a fit of dreaming

We were the freckled mark of Zorro,
robins hooded under Superman's cape,
Hopalonging Cassidy's on legs of whitehorses,
the Lone Ranger Social Club,
the Royal Canadian Air Force
bombing the Don with spit
and someone's running shoe

And what if a train came
and the Canadian Pacific or National Railroad
wiped our dirty faces and the rest of us away
What if we weren't afraid when it came, if it came,
and it rolled over us and kept rolling

Under tracks of nimble feet
and the steel scorching our toes,
the mud below that was water, and once, long ago,
welcomed great monarch-winged butterflies
and flesh-winged bathers — that mud
sucked in eyes until it stripped
all innocence of courage,
and we were left with nerves sweating
the last few parallel beams before ground

19

DOG AND BOY

Sport's the dog,
and the dog's mine
We run the fields together
Up hills
Down hills
Over and under
logs in the way

Sport jumps a stream
So do I
Dog and boy
jumping a stream

Sport says woof
and I say it too
Dog and boy
saying woof

I roll with Sport
all over the grass
We roll together,
dog and boy

Sport wears fur
I wear jeans
Otherwise, we look alike,
bark alike,
and howl at the full moon together

This boy's a dog
That dog's a boy
We take turns
being each other

Sport lifts his leg
to leak on a tree
I'd do the same,
but it hurts in jeans

Mosquitoes in his fur
Mosquitoes in my skin
We get stung together

When Sport gets fleas,
I get them too
We scratch together,
scratching fleas

Sport and me
on a rainy day,
we get wet together
When we dry
we stink the same
Stinking dog and boy

Sport's a mongrel,
a crossbred
blend of boxer,
collie, cocker spaniel and mutt
I've got Irish, Rumanian,
British and French
That makes me Canadian

Sport up to his snout
in a winter blizzard,
two yellow eyes
like peeholes
in the snow
until I dig him out
to take inside

A dog
too cold to walk,
or a dog
that likes being carried
Sport's one of these,
or maybe both

21

Wood burns
Stew stews
in a pot on the stove
A frozen dog
thaws by the heat
while the boy beside him woofs

Dog and boy,
that's Sport and me
I'm his pet,
and he's mine too

THE GIRL WITH THE YELLOW HAIR

The girl with the yellow hair
and skin paler than Mrs. Healey's white fence
gave you a cut-out valentine — two pink angels kissing
as they joined two halves of a red heart

You thanked her and put the valentine
into your back pocket,
where love was sure to be squished
with the other valuables
a kid carries into the battle of play

But thanks was not enough for her
She insisted on kissing you so hard
you were afraid she might smear your freckles
all over a face as red as the paper cut-out heart
she pressed into your freshly muddied hand

You wished you had not taken
the valentine from her, or offered thanks
You wished you looked
like Freddy Reed's younger brother, Werewolf Reed,
and could scare the girl with the yellow hair
paler than a bedsheet ghost, before halloween,
with just one growl of pointed teeth

You wanted to disappear
like the Invisible Man
when he was the Invisible Boy

When you learned that she could run faster
than you running as fast as jackflash,
you stopped while your breath still panted
and let her hug you and touch you
where Father McKillop said
it was bad to let other people touch you

And you wondered how to explain in confession
about getting hard whenever
the girl with the yellow hair
put her hand down the front of your pants
You wondered until your cousin told you
that certain things didn't need confessing

But how would he know?
He was a Protestant
and could get hard anytime
without feeling the need to confess

In the confessional, Father McKillop
told you to say three Hail Mary's
You said six to be sure

Three for tomorrow
when you would let the girl with the yellow hair
put her hand down to her elbow
because you promised her faithfully,
like a good Catholic
with his faith in the right place

THE NEWFY GIRL

In the garage one night raining,
the Newfy girl, salt cod
wherever he smelled her,
taught him, with skirt
lifted, how to taste her

Head squeezed between legs
warm as all the breath
that wet his throat, he thought
the falling sky and her were one

How else to explain
the little clap of thunder
that shook him to his feet
and mouth of cloud
that followed pouring

She shaped him lightning
in her hands, made his laughter
cut across the raging air
until her mother called
from a second floor window

Outside overhead, a light
dripping between roof boards
The gasp when she let go, left him
with nowhere but home
to take what she had built

TWELFTH AUGUST

August ripens more than berries this summer
These are your fields walking us into woods,
and you know their trails as I know
the streets I came playing from

I follow behind you, pick burs,
thistle from your dress
and hair with more strands of dark
than the trees that lean into our eyes

We are everywhere breathing,
are shadows made from touching,
air drinking from our throats
until they are dry and their only speech
is words undressed to nervous laughing

Your skin is darker than mine,
native to this soil
It tastes me tasting its scent,
oils from pores I fall into,
becoming your flesh,
its light and lovely power

DANNY'S TRACTOR

The day Danny took me out on the tractor,
two dogs followed, yelping

Butterflies swarmed from our path,
and I tried to snatch one
Its freedom for a moment to hold,
and wings, their fluttering,
to feel between closed palms,
gold and warming there

Across the heated grass to hotter field,
Danny, the dirt farmer's son, and me
took to sky and field with shirts off
Our skin sponged August, each furrow
sweated to overflow among the burning crops

I only knew the farm grew potatoes
I didn't know it grew cabbages and turnips and peas
And Danny didn't tell me about the work it took
to take food from the ground
Out on the tractor, it all came to me

Danny was half-breed, bred by the land,
and his dad had medals on the wall
from the Second World War

Their house was old boards, and it seemed
only the rust from the nails held it standing
lopsided on a hill, with seven kids to shelter

Danny alone needed space for five,
and his dad was tall and his mom was wide

The wood stove fed nine and guests
Beef broth at a boil, turnip limp,
and cabbage floating in the foam
You could smell it in the trees ten days later,
taste it in the air until a rainfall fell

Danny's skin didn't burn out on the tractor,
but my face steamed like stewed tomatoes
My back blistered and shed in the fields
My throat wanted a lemonade,
hand-squeezed by Danny's mom
and cold as brook water

THEY HUNG THE BAD MEN

On a grey morning, they hung the bad men

In the drizzle and rain,
after the blood and choking
at the end of two ropes,
we sat to dinner on a usual day

My father read it in the newspaper
as he spooned his soup at the table
We all heard it on the news, about two gangsters

It's another dark day with blood in it,
but we just live as usual
There's a comedy on at seven
Eddy's father got him two tickets
for the Maple Leafs on Saturday
I've never been to the Gardens before

The news said those gangsters
killed some people and robbed some banks
So I guess it's okay to kill them back
and take their lives Right?

The walls in this building are flimsy
My mother says you can hear everyone's business
Some nights in bed, I hear people
groaning through the walls and ceilings
I hear fights I hear crying,
and fists on the walls
What gets them angry?
Why is there so much trouble in people's lives?

I get angry when I see a kid getting hit
Nobody hits me in my home
Why do they have to hit kids?
It makes kids want to hit someone else,
someone smaller than them
— like when Ernie hit me in the schoolyard once

Ernie's dad beats him
So Ernie tortures cats,
and one day he'll kill someone to get even

We went to bed that night in the drizzle and rain
The weatherman said some sun tomorrow
Some sun's better than drizzle and rain

Eddy said the neck snaps
and the tongue sticks out
and they shit their pants when they're hung

The people upstairs are watching the late show
Don't they know there's a kid with school tomorrow?
Or were they never kids?
It's a western
I think I saw it ... the Indians get killed

My father's friend at work is Indian
I like Indians better than the U.S. Cavalry
Geronimo is my favourite
He only kills to defend his land and people
Indians have rights too

The late show is over
The national anthem is up loud
I'll hear it in class tomorrow

My teacher asked me what my nationality was
I said Canadian
No, he said, nobody's a Canadian
What does he mean nobody's a Canadian?
Eddy's a Canadian
My father's a Canadian,
and fought the Nazis in Italy
So did my uncle

You've got to fight the Nazis
when they're killing people and beating up kids
who just want to live as usual

Maybe my teacher means only Indians are Canadians
I'll ask him tomorrow when there's some sun
and the bad men they hung are buried and forgotten

EDDY AT THE INTERSECTION

Eddy's in a car
turning a corner behind my eyes

At this intersection
our lives go different ways,
but memories converge here,
stop in a traffic of days
for the red flickering candle
Eddy lit in his basement

Rhythm in the shadows, blues
in our faces, familiar streets
with a saxophone blasting,
known to the cry
that loves and hurts all at once

You don't forget a boy on skates
racing the sky across ice
that freezes in your mind

Eddy, breathless in his freedom,
leaving wind, clouds
and his best friend gasping

Only my heart could skate that fast,
fast enough to catch each beat
even while the winter
blew me all around,
knocked me ass-backwards
against the spray
Eddy's blades left in their wake

Flat on the ice,
I could laugh and call Eddy back
as if I were calling the wind
— and the small echo that froze in my mouth
was his name shouted to cut across the sky

Eddy comes back to the intersection,
our time in reverse, reversing the years
for another moment at the wheel
before we turned away
with different lives in mind

We flip the past like a coin
tossed and twirling to land
heads-up on a bet we both won

Call the toss both ways, heads
and tails somersaulting
down hills that roll away with boyhood
when we crash up against the sun
and squeeze laughter from its light
until the juices overflow

The year Eddy's father died
he learned about courage
while I didn't know what changed him,
what made the boy a man
or made his feelings
grow to fill that empty space

The intersection ahead
Eddy's engine revving
Mine on idle
Still a daydreaming boy
with his head in the sun

SINCE HE FELL FOR WANDA

It's October, almost November,
and Wanda's still on his mind

He's been playing Lenny Welch's
Since I Fell For you
all evening and into the night
Now the turntable turns inside him
and the needle cuts deeper,
each groove a wound
for that incredible voice to soothe

It's too bad, and it's too sad,
the silence between each play
Enormous quiet
with his heart in the middle spinning

Tears never taste their own salt
or feel the sting that cuts
They only know about falling,
as if that's all there is to being tears

Nothing is lit,
not the streets or the sky outside,
while Wanda plays on
like a moth taunting the flame

He touches her eyes with his
and sees only endings
Never beginnings
Time that stops at days
he tasted every breath she gave him
and thought each moment was forever

He knows it will always be her
Always that rainy street
at the end of dreaming

HER LAST WINTER

After Grandpa died,
Granny chopped wood for the wood stove herself
Even in snow, when the mornings froze below zero,
she'd muffle up and take the axe to winter

The cold cut Granny's chafed, beautiful face
like wood splinters puncturing the air
But she struck back Each whack of the blade
shattering that cathedral quiet in the trees

The upper branches rang from her blows,
and the streams and rivers
where I fished the summers
took each chop to their black current
and hurled it down to the marshes

Granny carried the wood in her arms
as she had carried children,
and fish from Newfoundland waters,
and grandchildren, and potatoes from her field,
and great grandchildren, and berries
plucked out of the woods
that bulged red with them in August

At my birth she gave me breath to live,
and I have never stopped breathing
or loving her heart in mine

That winter, the fire she gave to wood
would light her valley days, and nights
when memories closed in a breath away
Then the breath she took and turned to end
the night's long dream and longer, longer waking

THE AUNTS

They move in slow circles, the women,
their years amounting to lives and deaths
Remember the funerals and weddings

The children poured from them
as if their wombs were hatcheries
and the ocean needed filling,
or there were too few fish
in the waters for life to eat,
and the nets that cast in all the boys
and girls of their making
needed more than God could possibly give

In the sun, or rain, or clouded snow,
they worked the kitchens, cooked and sang
In the ice, or heat, or storms that passed,
they set the tables, served and spoke
words that food and fire brewed

Dark setting in, and dark taking
the lightest of lives to death,
but that was not the end of it

The processions were pauses only
for breath to catch the breathers at rest
in the long run it takes to hold the whole together

Up to their arms over shoulders, flung
into life, full force where the sun smacks your eyes
and every flavour tasted is them

You love these women because their strength
made all tender life stronger,
and the lives torn from a hold on earth
went knowing the fiery chains they snapped from

NAMES

We are only memories of ourselves,
ghosts that lived the blood
and warmed it with our music

We are only what we whisper now,
our time invisible, shadowed in when
— when love was easy, when we burned

We are pages folded back to then
when remembering was a moment away,
and we tossed back its days
like blankets on fire — our lives on fire,
time burning down with only its ashes now to taste

We are this mirror smashed against our years
These words that make our speech
cut themselves on flesh still felt
— still the noise we made with night
until it came down morning, still where we slept,
and, sleeping, touched quiet the smoke
that wrapped us in its flames

We are the nails drawn back from night,
the door flung open to empty wall
Nobody lives here any more

The curtains are drawn and taken away
with the lives that hung them high

All that remains is a photograph
The camera was sold, or left behind
You kept the picture, kept black
that moment white with sun
when you were only steps from holding,
and what we held was sudden always

No more coffee Our cups are empty
The snow outside waits for an explanation

But who can explain the silence that breaks us?
Who can tell us what happens to love
when dying gets in the way?
Who knows this cold that turns
like a beaten animal on its own heart
and eats the fire there for warmth?
Who can make words to speak for us now?

The tables are all empty but for ours
and the lovers' behind us — words, laughter,
the quiet between them shared

What have we made of remembering
when even the night forgets our names?

NIGHT IN THE GREEN MOUNTAINS
Vermont, 1981

Where they are their darkest green
in shadow caverns, the mountain grasses

Watershed mountains between Lake Champlain
and the Hudson and Connecticut Rivers

At dusk, light lowering until it sinks
beneath footsteps and is gone

Phantoms imagined in these hills
where the sky slopes into mind

The moon swoops in
Waters heard streaming to New Hampshire's border

Moon that meets Mount Ellen's peak through spruce
and fir along the "long trail" forest footpath

All that straddles or crawls the quiet
move wings and flesh beneath

One whiff of the noiseless sky
and I'm on my back among the grassy throngs

Fireflies bulge in a black sky
Wingbeats heard where the forest deepens

A docile fluttering in my chest
Nighthawks glide across my eyes
and are gone, gone, gone

GATINEAU CROW & BLACKFLY MORNING
Mont Saint Marie, Quebec

                    Crow
        calls

Two featheredtogether on a telephone cable

                    Grey sky
        blackbird
                    Grey sky

        Blackflies swarm

                    Crow
and mist,
        lowflying

                    Crow
on
a
wooden
fence,
                    two

        together flying

Morning messages,
        messengers
where needles prick
        the clouded air Thin,
                    thinning trunks
hilltop
down
to puddled roads

Water heard,
        hidden un-
        der tan-
        gle-crossed branches A stream over
        rocks

Blackflies in
my throat

Moss
clumped
over
rocks, dripping
what poured before light
came, I came

Coffee still steaming
in my blackfly mouth

Over the lake, wings
        calm as re-
versed there seen woods

I walk into sky and Gatineau hills, swim
        both

LENNOX & ADDINGTON
COUNTY PUBLIC
LIBRARY

I SWIM TO YOU

I swim to you, into
your morning blueberry mouth
Do I want some? some with yogurt?

Only from your lips, tongue feeding me
Only in these waters waist high
where we wade through eyes
while the light's first breath
closes between us, brings on sky

Food enough, my hungering hold on you
I'll eat and eat you
and stop only to swallow
I'll only let you go if you say, let go,
let it fly from this time to never,
let never deny that ever we loved

Stroking the chill from night,
underwater Purple purposeful lips
around and through me, stroking

The waters to your table
and waters to your bed
What are the waters without us?

At the end of another beginning,
without lies to tell
Stripped to ourselves,
touch tells all from shore to heart
where no distance interrupts

Glide into me
Let others skim the waters,
take surfaces for a ride,
and others cool the flesh of air
while we set fire to all
that needs our burning

Love without us
is one love less

DAY IN AN UNDERTOW
Gulf of Mexico, 1990

The Caribbean tugs me
under turquoise swells,
or it might be the tequila

Gulls soar overhead,
sun bleaching their wings
in flight, in indigo light,
out where the whitecaps writhe

The beach hut shades me
Face in the sand
A foot in the sun

My dark beauty
on a white coral beach
Tonight she is mine
next to the quarter moon waters
I'll open her for the night to rage,
and we'll close together
when dolphins leap at dawn
out where the sea and sky are one

THE FLIP SIDE OF NIRVANA

THE FLIP SIDE OF NIRVANA

I never sang to the back street Sweet Marie
She had steel guitar ears
& could only hear Chuck Berry
riding along in his automobile
even while the radio played Blueberry Hill

The late show on the street
starred midget wrestlers
& the Friday night hotel fights
in technicolour

Chips & gravy &
a strawberry milkshake
to wash down Little Richard
who ripped up the jukebox
5 plays for 25 & no Beethoven

Schoolyard rock in white socks
Jerry Lee rolled
'em down
like hotel condoms, balling fire
in a backseat
while the Killer won again
on the flip
side of nirvana

Kerouac, James Dean & Rompin Ronnie
Howl hauled down
the beaten stars
& stoned them under
flight of foot

Whiter than pale
our eyes behind
cinemascopic shades Beaming up

JOHN'S GRILL BOOGIE
Sometime in 1955, or '56

How can I eat with Elvis in my soup?
dining on the John's Grill spec-i-al

When the greased pompadour
jives through the door,
you know it's Johnny
& he's out to black some eyes
or do a little cutting

I'm in mid-nibble on a soda cracker
when Leggy Mona bluejean's by my booth
& smiles her teeth in at me

You get 5 for a quarter on the jukebox,
& each of them is Elvis if you're Mona
— & if you're not, maybe Frank Sinatra,
but never Perry Como,
when you're combed to rock
& your socks is itching

Johnny itches to bite & kick
with a razor blade in his shoe
& attitude that needs a haircut

Mona slips under Johnny's arm, blows a bubble
like none's been blown before, & says
        Johnny, will you boogie with me?

I'm into my third spoon of soup
when the guests from Heartbreak Hotel
mob through the door demanding banquetburgers,
chips&gravy, hotbeef & col-l-l-l-l-l-ld peas,
COCOnutcreampie & limejello-o-o-o-o-o-o

Johnny finds a face he don't know in the crowd
& shouts *I wanna cut you*

I break another soda cracker
& do some salt in my soup
while the blood squirts around me

Mona spins on a stool, says she wishes
it was a horse or something

The ambulance arrives
with a stretcher & a siren
Johnny's eating raisin pie at the counter
with a kid whose stolen coat someone stole
while he was performing tricks
in the cold storage washroom downstairs

A policeman with a jaw
that has a law of its own
stops & speaks with Johnny,
asks him if he cut the victim

Johnny says *No, I don't even know the dude*

Nobody witnessed anything,
& my face is in soup,
blowing green pea bubbles

Meg, the sequin-haired waitress,
mops the blood from the floor
& asks me how the soup was, says

    John always uses salt pork & a ham bone

    SALT PORK & A HAM BONE?
    Sounds like you said SALT PORK & A HAM BONE, Meg, I say

    That's what I said, Meg says
    I said SALT PORK & A HAM BONE
    John always uses SALT PORK & A HAM BONE
    in his pea soup spec-i-al

That's what I thought you said
in the first place, Meg, I say

What'd you say? Mona asks Meg
when she stops to lipstick her breath

I said SALT PORK & A HAM BONE, Mona

Meg, did you say SALT PORK & A HAM BONE?

That's right Mona, SALT PORK & A HAM BONE

Even Johnny laughs, saying
SALT PORK & A HAM BONE

The cast from Heartbreak Hotel
get in the laugh as well,
& we all shout *SALT PORK & A HAM BONE*

Johnny & Mona jive to *SALT PORK & A HAM BONE*
until the bones are done on their feet,
& Mona proposes to Johnny
  Johnny, will you marry me?

Lifting his collar, he pushes open
the door to John's Grill
& slinks out onto the pavement, saying
  Yeah, Mona, when the welfare office freezes over

CANADIAN CLUB

A maple down, stump
uprooted Low nimbostratus
darken the narrow back road,
where last night's snow filled ruts
in the tire-gutted gravel

Wings disappear into the field,
steep with brush that thickens
against a shapeless sky,
reappear when a dog barks
down the wind, dead rabbit
running in its jaws, ears aflap

Hills ahead, only a purple mist
beyond the downward slope of road

A dog crawls the marsh
Fenceposts jut toward ...

Gunshot Wings in a rush overhead

Radio up the hill plays Elvis
louder with approaching wheels
Are you lonesome tonight?

The man behind the windshield chews dentine
Yesterday's news on his lap
Canadian Club in the glove compartment
Six condoms in a package on the dash

She stands in the window
behind striped curtains

The nose of a Chevy
on the incline ahead

Snow slashes past her face in the pane

Another gunshot He slams the car door

A rabbit drops to steel-toed boots,
saliva on its bloodied neck

She rides him
while the sky collapses
and the night is head-long — a white storm coming

Hexagonal stars in a wooded galaxy,
crystal as their hands that reach
past each breath unspoken

GEORGE'S BILLIARDS & SNACK BAR

What can you say about pool hall boys
when the girls don't want to know them?

A masculine cue is all they need
for that shot in the corner pocket

What can I tell you about the boys
down at George's Billiards & Snack Bar?

It's another Saturday night
and only the cue balls are polished

Ask me if they'd rather be mating
than chalking their tips for a shot

I'd say chalking their tips for a shot
because mating's not in their nature

If you need to know what *is* in their nature,
just ask and I'll explain their disposition

They're boys' boys ... simple as that
Just like George is a man's man

If you're asking me what the pool hall boys
do for a little excitement, don't

Don't ask because I'm liable to tell you,
and you probably know already

But if you need to know what gets the boys going,
I'll have to use language to answer that one

And there's no language allowed at George's
The sign taped on the wall says so

But if you come in the back to the washroom,
I'll show you what gets the boys going on the wall

It's all there to see in its epigraphic entirety
George gave up trying to erase those stubborn locutions

These are real fantasies, poolhall wet dreams
Obscene, yes, except for the odd philosophic saying

Are there pool hall philosophers? Do they really exist?
Or are they strictly a mythical breed?

I'd have to say both, mythical and real,
and leave it to your imagination

The authors of these illiterary works
wish to maintain their anonymity

Anyone who asks me to name names, I won't
Let's keep this confidential, please

You don't see nothing that happens in George's
The rent money you walk out without, you walked in without it too

Possibly you lost it at the racetrack, or donated it
to the church of your religious persuasion

This guy whose name I won't name, and don't inquire ...
he took a pool cue across the shoulder blades

Why? Why did he take a pool cue across the shoulder blades?
I'm not saying, and you won't get a word from me

I mean you could get a word from me
I can be encouraged to talk

But don't ask me down at George's,
where language is kept to a minimum unless you're George

You can talk your way into the back alley,
and you'll need your lips stitched at emergency

Are there gangs down at George's?
Your guess could be as good as mine

But if we're guessing, I'd guess yes
Yes, there are gangs down at George's

What do these gangs call themselves,
especially since none are incorporated?

I'd have to be definitely vague and say,
there's devils and snakes in their names

But not all the pool hall boys get into gangs
Some are loners who only mix with their moms

Are there other pool halls in the neighbourhood? Yes, two
There's Hollywood Billiards & Snack Emporium up the street

It's rumoured they have a better class of pool player,
boys in two piece suits and shiny ties wearing Brut cologne

Then there's Snooker's five blocks away,
but nobody goes there ... It's too crowded

If you don't like George's, and the honest truth is some don't,
I can recommend certain uptown establishments

I sometimes play at the Coronation Billiard Academy,
but don't you go expecting to meet *the* Queen

Then there's LaParisienne Bistro & Billiards
where the players call themselves billiardists

Billiardists frown on snooker, but the way I see it
there's six pockets and a slate table whatever game you play

They serve fifty-five kinds of coffee at La Parisienne's,
but down at George's it's coke coke coke from the coke machine

If you ask me what sort of snacks are served at George's,
I'd suggest you ask George instead

Order a hot dog, and he'll talk over mustard
After the mustard, he'll talk over relish

George will really talk over his fresh cut onions
because he's proud they don't come frozen from McCains

George will tell you, all the inedibles come frozen
over at the Hollywood Billiard & Snack Emporium

Frozen pizza with sub-zero pepperoni
Icicled nachos with chilled jalapenos

George's pizza is baked by Mrs. George,
and his daughter Theresa does the ham & salami subs

It's all fresh, George will tell you
Even the eggs pickle themselves in a pickle juice jar

That's George   That's George's Billiards & Snack Bar
What more can I say?   Don't ask, or I might tell you

SHOWERING WITH GREG

Showering with Greg
in a discount bath house
25 cents for soap and towel

All that dirt from the streets washing off
There goes last night
in a froth down the drain

Dundas & Yonge foaming in the armpits
Goodbye Dundas & Yonge

And lower Jarvis Street tavern,
glasses on glasses of draft ...
there you go, pissed against the wall,
sucked and swallowed away

The Melody Club from midnight to dawn,
switchblade inferno with a rock & roll beat
Now it splashes in a lather from your head

Rolling home-grown on the beach
Seeds crackle at six a.m.,
sun rising where your eyelids fall
underwater in a spray — sand
and the stench of dead, bloated fish
flushed from your skin

Greg's well hung, but down
to a drizzle, hanging low

You're down to bubbles
popping in your ears

A little towel fight to prove
there's still some child in both of you

Two effervescent boys
on the bath house steps,
cleansed for the streets to dirty again

RELEASED FROM WAWA
for Chris Faiers

Snowbound in Tim's old Chevy
on the ice-skirts of Wawa,
highway headlights smeared
across our smoked-out eyes

No room in the sky for another flake
to fall on our soft white heads

Automobile down
Windshield avalanched
Footprints in the storm
make bleak eternity on a head of wind,
drift from each bootstep
that follows its flight on dusk-blue wings

We circle ourselves,
blow breath into red hands,
shake them against the stinging air
and zombie-walk into town

My boots crunch across the railway platform,
and I imagine a train — light paling
on tracks the distance of dream

I imagine money for a ticket,
see my face warming against windows
that race the frost-blurred sun
— Canadian Club in the club car
and a notebook of un-
finished poems in my coat

I reserve a seat on the platform bench
and travel nowhere until my ass gets chilled

We kick the stars from our boots
and step into the local hotel

There is no gold in the snow outside
It's all under foam
in a blizzard of beer blowing across the tables
Jack, with three-hundred pounds of blanched face,
peels the skin back from his eyes
and shows us where he was hiding

Loraine confesses she has nothing to say,
except, yes, she'll accept another round

Blotto is not his name ... It's Bill
But all the same they call him Blotto
ten glasses before he blanks out snoring

Jean Ellen lashes out at Loraine,
kicks under the table until she finds a knee

I look out the window
Cold bites five reflections of my face
I try to hide the other four,
but Jean Ellen is talking to each of them
while the one that scares me most
is fixed on a glacier sliding by the window

Twenty-two year old Tommy,
with gravel in his spit,
wants to arm wrestle,
asks me while I choke on my glass
and suggest he tries Blotto ... or Loraine

Harold limps in with icicled lips,
beats his mitts to submission
and orders a Black Label

There is no more room at the table
But Sandy leans between Blotto and me
Eight people on four chairs
She finds a lap and collapses
against my unfinished poems

I must find an unfinished publisher
when I am released from Wawa

THE STARS IN HIS ARM

Coffee at the counter
A clean ashtray
The lame kid drops
a bundle of newspapers
inside the door

The sun is on the street
It won't be long
before we disappear
into another day

Two cabbies
and a girl with smeared eyes
find a booth and discuss
last night's tragedy

Bobby passes the sugar
I look at my face in the spoon
Something isn't right
I turn to Bobby,
show him the spoon, say
Do I Look right in this spoon?
Bobby takes it from my hand
and looks at himself instead

Two men with bibles
bulging in their briefcases
talk through the door
One is a block
under his brush of head
No neck
His face is redder
than the cherry pie
his pimple-faced friend
orders with orange juice
I guess him three-hundred
pounds of sanctimonious sweat

I inhale steam from the cup
The man at the end of the counter sings to himself
Another talent for whom the world is not waiting
I don't know if his eyes are lost
or if they're found or if it matters,
but they're looking at Bobby and me
and I can't get comfortable

An old lady with potted fern in hand
finds a table in the corner
and orders water for her friend

I stir cream into my coffee
The steam settles and I taste it
with one eye on the man now singing at us

Someone's ordered toast
Knife in a block of butter
behind the counter — thin wedges
sliced and scraped onto a plate

The man talks at us
He could be somewhere in space
on a mission unknown even to himself
How can five stools away be that far?
Bobby and him are talking

A young man with a tuba in his arms
pushes past the crowd coming in, shouts
>   *Breakfast special again, Sam*
>   *Eggs over easy and don't forget,*
>   *wheat toast, Sam ... wheat toast*

>   *I remember, Timmy,* says Sam
>   *Yesterday I forget, but today*
>   *I remember Wheat toast for Timmy*

Are those bugs
floating in my cup?
I show Sam
He says coffee grounds

I put my face down
into the cup, say
     Are you sure?

       Yeah, coffee grounds Want another?

I poke Bobby
     Bobby, you have grounds in your coffee?
     If you have coffee grounds
     Sam'll give you another cup

Bobby says no, but he's distracted,
so I look in his cup to make sure
     Yeah, he's got grounds as well, Sam
     We'll both have another coffee

A blind man pokes his cane
through the door, tugs
on a leash, hauls
his dog in behind him

I'm listening to Bobby and the man
It's something about the weather
Cloud conditions
Degrees of heat
It rained yesterday
He tells Bobby
he found an umbrella on the subway,
but it had a hole in it
Bobby laughs
He laughs as well

64

What's it like for him?
ten million lights years
from the stars in his arm,
being a time traveller without a watch,
lost among people with umbrellas
who holiday in Muskoka,
buy their lives on time
and hope one day to live them,
have social insurance numbers
to assure them they are social,
play scrabble with dictionaries on their laps,
and only fly Air Canada

Bobby says Let's go
We fly through the door
Only we are amazed

CORNER MAN

If it's a fast
up
and down
game,
I'm lost

I can't keep up
Nothing worse

I don't skate
I struggle

I play
how I look,
broken nose
and all

I outwork
the opposition,
hustle in
the corners

I don't have the big ego

I know what I can
and can't do

I forget
how many time
my nose
get broken

I'm hit
with deflection
three game in a row

I broke
my jaw
in Chicoutimi
and had to wear
a mask after that

It's just a job
It feeds
my family

Even a guy like me,
he can do well

POEM WITH A DOG UP ITS ASS

Bare, the branches
Grey, the squirrel
The day white as birch
Birch warmed by dim light,
shaft of winter sun
The tangled sky

Old maple bark, rugged trunk
Cables strung above the yards
where fenced-in tables ladders plastic pools
gas barbecues and chrome chairs are scattered
among left-over lawns, disposable grass

Leaves on the ground
past green
past yellow
past any discernible colour
Take a vacuum cleaner to them
Take a broom or take a rake

Always a daylight dog barks
There's one barking now
Take a gun to it
Take a baseball bat or take a bone
Shoot it club it or feed it

Silence that dog by any means
Feed it to its master
Get that dog out of this poem
Get a cat instead
A cat crossing a fence, hanging
from a telephone cable,
or sleeping outside a cold closed window
A cat crying at the door
It wants in
Once in it wants out
Once out it'll be back
once the dinner tin is opened

Open the door for the cat
Open the poem for the cat

Kick the dog out
Let it run wild in the streets
If it's good enough for crazed drugged humanity,
it's worthy of a dog whose only crime
is the fool who owns it in his or her image

If only their masters
could master a squirrel, or a poem
without a dog's interference
These people will never read
a poem without a dog in it
They demand doggerel,
and this poem is not about to stoop
any more than they scoop their canine shit
from public sidewalks parks and beaches

I told my neighbour I'd maim his dog
if it snapped at me again
It did, and there is one less
loose brick in my house
and one more dog's jaw in the ass of my poem

FIRE & BRIMSTONE

Sperry, the local oddball poet,
listens up a tornado
when Fire & Brimstone,
the doom-saying donut shop visionary,
sends tremors through our coffee cups
THERE'S A CATACLYSM COMING he says

But when I look out the window
all I see is us reflected there
Four men — two working on coconut crullers,
one with permanent statue of liberty eyes,
& the other whose designs on hell
is giving everyone heartburn

It's 2 a.m., & this abyss of sugar
— double with double cream in your mud caffeine,
or all over your honey dipped donut —
this pit of bottomless cups & worthless burps,
this netherworld of nether-to-be's,
this ectoplasmic plastic hole in the yeast inferno,
this donut shop is cursed

It don't matter if you microwave your meat pie,
& it don't count if you only sinned once
in the last fifteen minutes,
& Fire & Brimstone don't care
if you're a card carrying Progressive Conservative
— you're going to hell on the ass end of a tornado

You'll have three days of darkness
to get your head on straight,
& there won't be no mirrors for cheating
You'll have three days of darkness, & that's all,
to get your shit together & march right out into Paradise,
out your front door, three days later,
& shout so's the angels can hear you
HEY, WHAT SIDE'S UPSIDE DOWN?

You'll be confused at first,
when everything appears reversed
or sideways, or otherwise on an angle

You'll stop by the same donut shop
that got you cursed in the first place, & look inside
You'll see the waitress balancing spoons on her ankles
Jelly donuts will float by,
& for the first time in your life you won't want one
because them jelly donuts is exPLODING

After them three days of darkness,
when you go outside & get a whiff of Paradise,
you'll wish you'd listened to Fire & Brimstone
when he spoke about all them people
having cataclysmic visions in their backyards,
on their doorsteps & the local donut shop

People was having ugly visions everywhere
They saw frogs falling from the heavens
& warts not far behind
They saw a man's collection of plastic ducks
turn on him whilst he was asleep
& peck his head until it bled with feathers
They saw all manner of ugly things

There were prophecies of doom
& predictions of gloom,
but nobody told us
Ignorance is blissful & we was blissed
We was blissed until Fire & Brimstone
told us about damnation

Now we believe in miracles
We have visions too
We're not scared

HERE'S LOOKING AT BOGIE, SWEETHEART

Bogie's my man, Sweetheart
Now take it & like it
& if you don't like it,
I'll fondle my own ear lobe

I suppose you'll say
like Captain Renault in Casablanca,
    You're a rank sentimentalist

But as time goes by, you'll see ...
the harder the shell the softer the heart
That's what makes Bogie Bogie
Moral ambiguity on a tough face

There's hostile forces everywhere, Kid,
& you need the wit of a Rick or Sam Spade
to torpedo your way through like the African Queen

It all began at the Black Mesa Filling Station & Bar-B-Q
I'd just ordered ham & petrified eggs
when Duke Mantee put a gun to my head
I swung around on the stool
expecting to see Bette Davis eyes,
but saw puffed-up despair instead, & I said,
    I've killed men for looking at me like that

Duke snarled back,
    Who'd you expect, Shirley Temple?

"Rocks" Diamond is my man, Angel
So's Chips Maguire & Roy "Mad Dog" Earle
Three cheap hoodlums who hang around hotel lobbies
with heaters in their clothes
These guys don't slap so good in the evening,
but they all know how to whistle
They just put their lips together & blow

Philip Marlowe & me are like two hills of beans, Angel
& neither of us looks like a pekinese
that sits on people's laps
while they're standing up

It comes to me like a photograph against the eyelids
I was wearing a trench coat the night I met Bogie
We stopped on a rainy street
to light each other's cigarette

Bogie scowled in the headlights of cars
with black & white windshields & said,
   Quit your stalling & stop biting your thumb

I took the thumb from my mouth
& Bogie flipped a coin into my hand as if to say
   Here, Pal, buy yourself a cigar

Now you're wise to where I was
last night in the rain, Sweetheart
I was with a private dick on a public street
We went to the Blue Parrot Bar
& swapped shots between drinks
& drinks between shots

Bogie liked his rye with more rocks than San Quentin
He chased it down with a martini
while I had a double Shirley Temple & a straw

I tapped Bogie's glass with mine & said,
   Here's to plain talking
   I'm a man who likes talking
   to a man who likes talking

But he warned me,
   People lose teeth talking like that

So I asked him,
> *Do you want me to learn how to stutter?*

> *No,* he said, *just stop talking like a sap*

It looked like the beginning of a beautiful friendship
when Bogie confessed,
> *A private dick is just a guy*
> *who's paid to do other people's laundry*

This stuff about people's laundry didn't wash with me
I wanted to know why a private dick came so cheap
Only twenty-five dollars a day & expenses
I don't object to a parasite
I just object to a cut-rate one

Bogie squinted from the smoke that closed his eyes
until they were the size of the olives in his martini

I sipped hard on my fifth Shirley Temple
but the suction made my dimples cave-in,
& my jaw just collapsed on the bar

That's when Bogie said,
> *Don't go simple on me*

But I complained
> *Of all the Shirley Temple joints*
> *in all the towns in all the world,*
> *I have to lose my dimples here*

THE MILLER'S UFO

Story goes Old Jack,
parked in his pick-up
out on the church road,
had a bottle to his mouth
(apricot brandy, I'm told)
when he saw this light
bigger than a barn
turning & turning
in the sky overhead

Old Jack swallowed
half the bottle there & then,
not taking his eyes
from what appeared like a ferris wheel
with red & green lights
that flashed off & on again
& landed in the Miller field
out back of Smiley Lake

I heard Old Jack got out of his truck
armed with a shotgun,
stomped through the bush,
over a fence,
past the meadow
& down to the field
where he saw a spaceship
land next to the Miller house

All the Millers
except 11 year-old Amy
got in the spacecraft

She took off on her bicycle
while her dad, standing next to a creature
with a head the size of a pumpkin,
shouted for her to come back

That's when the creature,
with one eye blinking
in the middle of its face,
aimed a hand at Amy

An orange ray
shot through the air
& struck the girl, who disappeared

Old Jack was about to fire
at the one-eyed pumpkin-headed creature
when he saw Amy reappear next to her mom,
who stood at the door of the spaceship
waving good-bye to their dog, Liliput,
& their cat, Jerome

A terrific racket followed
as the spacecraft lifted off
with the Millers aboard
& Old Jack blasting
his shotgun after it,
& Liliput barking
& Jerome up on his hind legs hissing

Old Jack denies this story,
& most everybody agrees
it don't explain why the Millers
would just get up & take off in a UFO
when George Miller won big
in the provincial lottery
only seven weeks ago
& Maud Miller
had a trip to Florida planned

Old Jack's drinking buddy, Ralph,
got the story going only a week after
the Miller's disappearance

Ralph claims Old Jack told him
over a jug of suds
down at the Crescent Moon Motel
how he saw the Millers
leave of their own free will in a spaceship

The Miller's disappearance
remained a mystery until last week
when Ralph received a postcard from Maud
saying the family had settled
in the Bermuda Triangle
& they missed everyone, especially
Old Jack Liliput Jerome Ralph & the gang
down at the Crescent Moon Motel

Ralph persisted with his UFO story,
claiming Old Jack told him
a spaceship flew the Millers
down to the Bermuda Triangle
where they were electro-magnetized
& entered a future time-zone
know only to mystics,
extra-terrestrials
& progressive conservatives

TWAIN'S COMET

You rode in on a comet,
said you'd leave the same way
— saddled to Halley's back

"Two unaccountable freaks"
alarming the night with your flames

You went out on Halley's steamboat,
riding fire like the wild Mississippi,
old stogey smoking up a tempest
in your mouth still chomping sparks

There must've been a Tom
idling under the lazy moon
the night you charted
your course through the stars
— and he must've heard you
pacing the stage, his imagination,
where them wildest dreams come true

There must've been a Huck leaping
like the Calaveras County frog from his raft
for Halley's fireworking tail,
to grab on for a ride

And he must've heard you
shouting "Hang on, Huck,
when waves as large as the moon,
in circles and crescents of light,
spun him two fathoms deep
down the longest river that ever piloted the night

THE DEATH OF LI PO

Dream-spirited Po,
you reach for her on the waters,
think she is the moon reflected there,
and fall — you fall, Li Po, out of your boat

Wine-singing Po,
you reach into mist,
grapes splitting on your tongue
Vines bulge erected from your wings
flopping where your heart glides
into her face of ghost and waters

O Po Li Po
O you embrace illusion
You hold her to your drowning chest
and squeeze her life from your head

O Po Li Po
O you lunge for her breasts,
her grapes to taste
all nippled wet and China gold

O Po Li Po
You drunken dog of a poet barking at death

Li Po,
your eyes are rolling
They swim in your head
to a shore where the ground is never,
the grasses dance with invisible crickets,
shells from the sea echo forever,
shipwrecked lives sail the dark sands
and she is the lantern
swinging from an unknown height

Li Po Li Po,
her star-clustered moon
opens for man and poem and wonder

O Po,
you choke on wonder,
swallow the curve of her light,
cry laughter in bubbles that break,
singing on the blue current
you pump your chest against, O Po

Po,
into these rhythms you go,
your throat choking on its swollen tongue

O Po, Li Po, you ancient beast

ESENIN'S SUICIDE

Esenin, slice your wrists
into these lines that dissect your voice,
cut pieces of flesh from your words
and this poem will know you as bleeder,
as the blood that soaks its paper flower

Esenin, these are your wrists —
sticks I snap for the sounds they make
snapping hollow when they break on wisdom,
each piece no longer a hand on this page

Esenin, this language drinks from veins
Do you? Do you still drink
at the curve of your hand into song?
Bloodlet, Esenin, bloodlet your throat
hung singing from a rope,
and dance once more with Isador choked

Sharpen the blade, Esenin
Sharpen those rhythms that empty you,
spill images, pools in red ink
here where the poem waits for your suicide

Now only the light obscured
Only your face squeezed pale

Choke on this, Esenin,
the pulse shredded into each beat
and the truth told backwards, told
bleeding back on the heart,
its hind legs kicking at love

Come into this slit, Esenin,
where the masters sit, voices gathering
in the great alone, where language is the cage
we smash and sing against our freedom

Dangle here, Esenin, hang
from this stanza that stands you
draining into its last word

SHAUNT BASMAJIAN: A CLASS PRODUCTION

Water chopping our voices
at Ashbridges Bay

We took beer
down to the rocks,
uncapped them with words
intoxicating the mute, humid air

His voice on the secluded water
spoke from a heart
too big for one life to fill,
but large enough for the ghosts
that took flight from its beating wings

Hurt was another of his names
That's how the blues
came to know this Armenian,
driving through streets
that got him knifed
in his taxi one night

Life tipped him
four more years,
but he told me the nightmare he slept
— his blood again
in courtroom pictures

It was Fern in his words
that night with temperate breezes
crossing the lake,
another love lost to losing
Beautiful Fern,
not ready for a man
whose hold on his soul
would never hold her,
a boy on a limb
looking to fall,
the poet whose wounds
time or her touch
could never heal

After the beer bottomed out,
a holocaust on his mind
— his words burning the lake
where sky and water
met to take him down
with all the deaths of his people

I asked him to write it,
not knowing he already had
in the arms of other broken lovers,
in forsaken bars on lonely streets
that rocked with his song
to the beaten and lost
— that inferno he spoke of,
his heavy music,
and words gentle from the child

BUILDERS OF TEMPLES
Cancun, Mexico, 1990

At five a.m.
the workers straggle
onto the tin bus,
mostly young men
with sleep
still hanging
from their eyelids,
not wanting to let go

They carry their sleep
inside, bundled in eyes
that look back at the dark
through windows, while
their dreams recede
into waking
when the door
clangs shut
and the engine
rattles through bone
and rusted tin

Today as yesterday
and tomorrow,
they build temples
for the rich tourists
The gods no longer matter
The gods are dead
in this wasteland of wealth
where cranes hoist
marble and concrete
into the Yucatan sun

Their faces are soft,
boys still gentle with love
where their muscles ache
They left their homes,
came here to work
and build the hotels
for big foreign money
that drips down
to their foreheads
a drop at a time,
much slower
than tequila

Others peddle in the streets ,
hustle the rich tourists
No welfare cheque waiting
at the end of a broken line
Their spirits must rise,
or they'll fall beneath
the feet of others
out to make those pesos

DAYBREAK AT LOS APACHES CAFÉ
San Antonio, Texas, 1992

It's daybreak at Los Apaches Café
The sun's between the cracks on the sidewalk outside
— a splinter of the day to come
You think you'll leave it there ... looks all right

Avocado-green booths
stuffed with faces that talk the day into action
Under the low-slung ceiling, coffee bangs against your eyes
Plates and teeth rattle with forks

You're reminded of the Ontario Diner in Toronto
Switch peak caps for white cowboy hats, and you've got it
All the characters, down-and-outers, people
whose dreams were beaten from them a day at a time
until their lives went on hold
These are the real beatniks

Later, you'll take in the Alamo up the street,
where you know they'll say John Wayne
and Davey Crockett won the West
But you came to Los Apaches Cafe
for eggs and the unofficial history of the Alamo

You glance at the old man in the next booth
The past is all over his face, and you figure he'll know
So you ask, "What really happened that day in 1836,
on February 23rd, when General Santa Anna
led four thousand troops against 187 men,
including John Wayne, Davey Crockett and Jim Bowie?"

The old man tells you they surrendered and were executed
They didn't go down fighting at all
(Huh, I knew it)

You connect with the waitress
She's not much taller than your knees,
but makes up for it in other directions
Her smile knows you, and the compliment is returned
Shit, there's only one race in this world, and it's us

So she asks what you want, and you tell her the eggs
Eggs will get you through today into tomorrow
Let the middle-class worry about cholesterol
Leave the eggs for those who know how to slop into them
Y'all need a little yolk on your face
to get life's taste sensation
Everyone's stuffing scrambled into their tortillas

You order the eggs, and spiced beef picadillo
A bowl of salsa verde on the table
— serrano chiles, the serious ones
One teaspoonful will blow out your ear drums,
peel your tongue, and smear your eyes across the floor
At the Ontario Diner, everyone pastes their eggs with ketchup
But you won't hear me running down ketchup

Three men and a woman at the next table
are rinsing their omelets with beer
You order a Lone Star to launder your eggs too

The sun's through the window where you sit
President Bush is giving a speech at the Alamo today
You expect to see Brian Mulroney
standing next to him in a coonskin cap
like the one John Wayne wore before he surrendered

LENNOX & ADDINGTON
COUNTY PUBLIC
LIBRARY

Ted Plantos was born in Toronto. *Mosquito Nirvana* is his ninth collection of poetry. He is the former publisher and editor of Cross-Canada Writers' Magazine. Currently, he co-ordinates the Milton Acorn Memorial People's Poetry Award.

"It is through discipline that he finds his voice. Plantos' lesson tells us that the most beautiful poetry is the poetry of the will."

– Alexandre L. Amprimoz, Quarry

"Plantos' work has the qualities of both pioneer poetry and social realism."

– Books in Canada

"... a real talent for narrative, and at his very best – when he is being witty, fantastic, or subtly sardonic – his poetry exhibits a marvellous variety and plasticity."

– Robert Casto, Waves